AIR ON THE G STRING
from ORCHESTRAL SUITE NO. 3

HORN

By Johann Sebastian Bach

EINE KLEINE NACHTMUSIK

HORN

By Wolfgang Amadeus Mozart